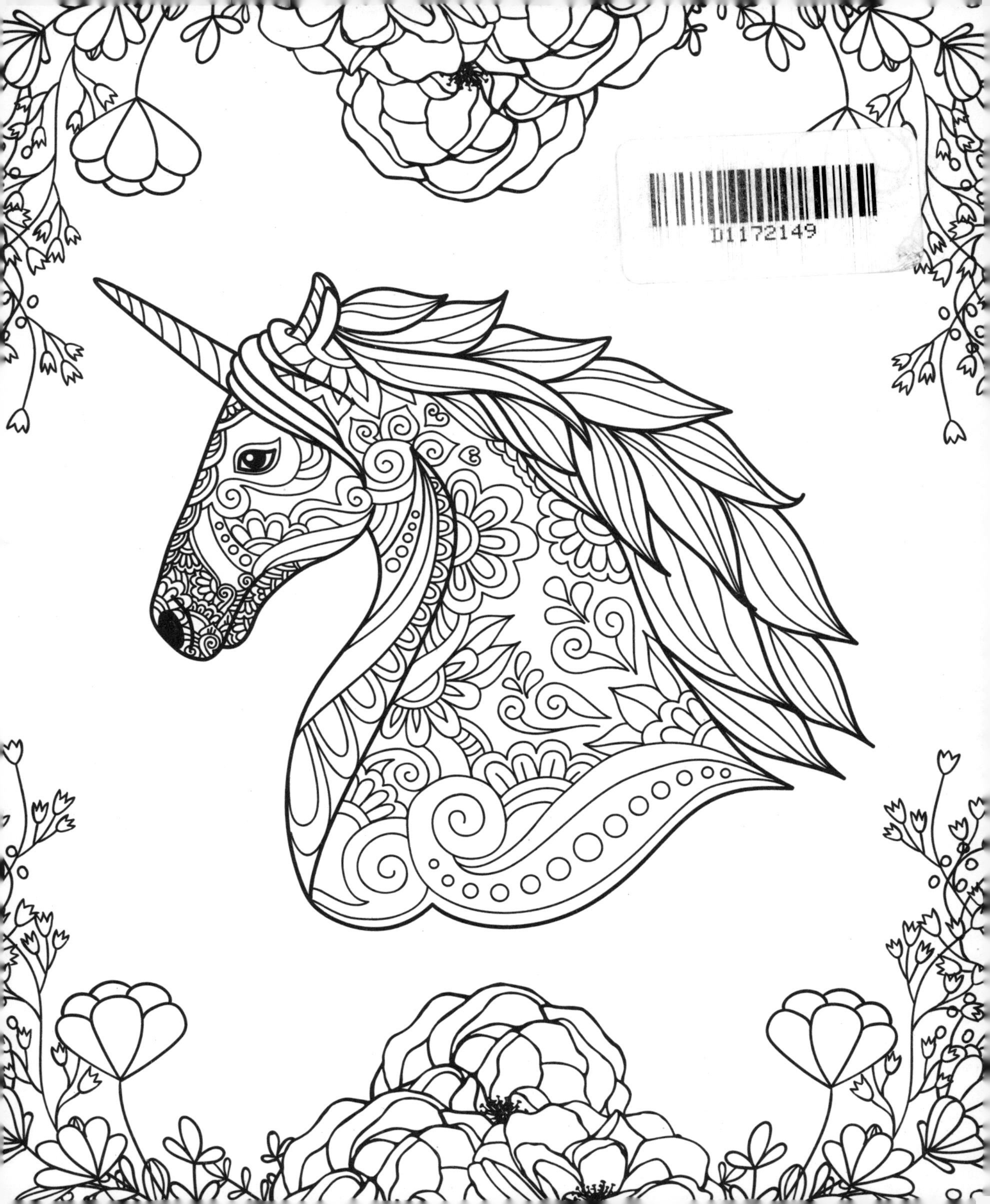

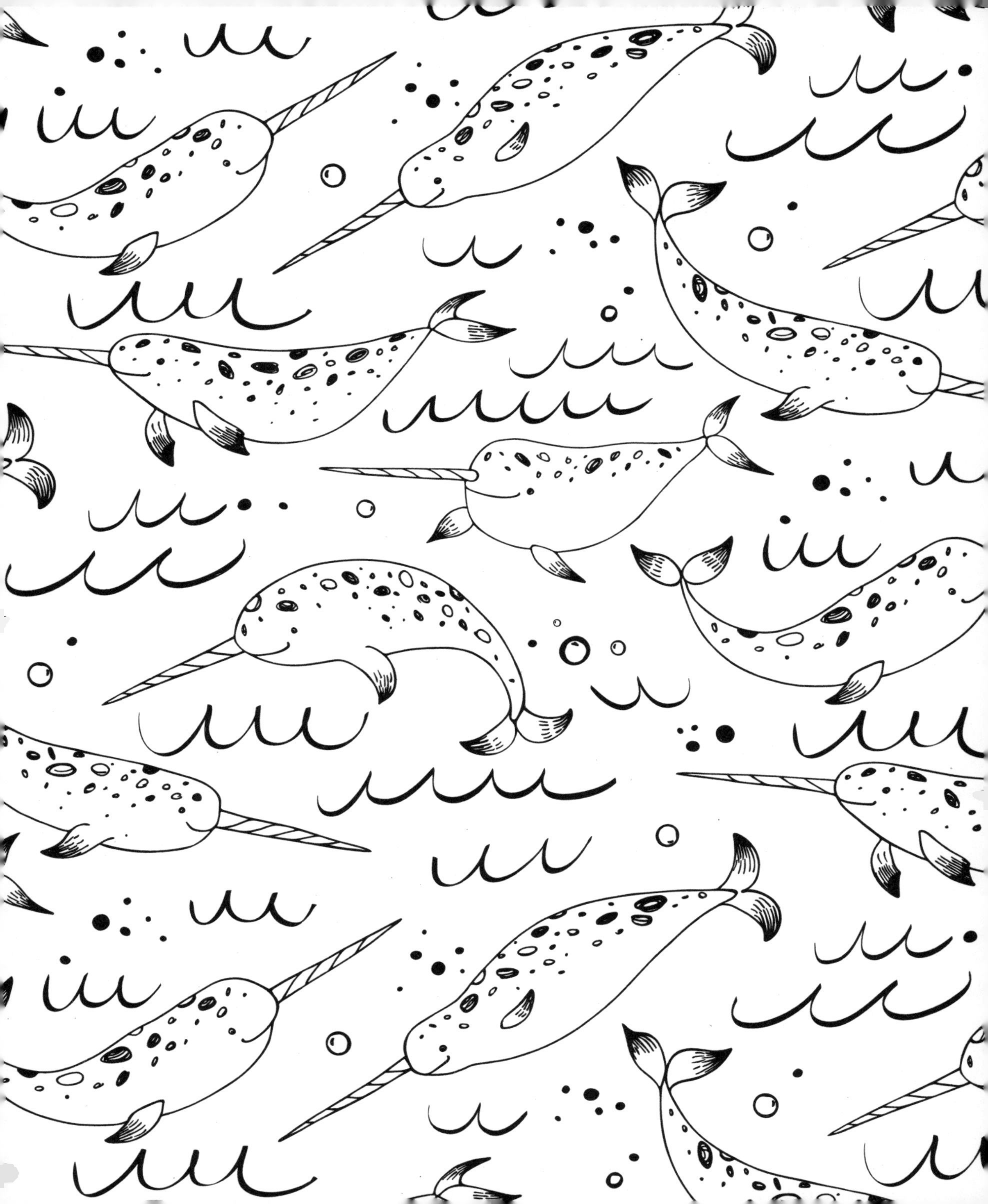

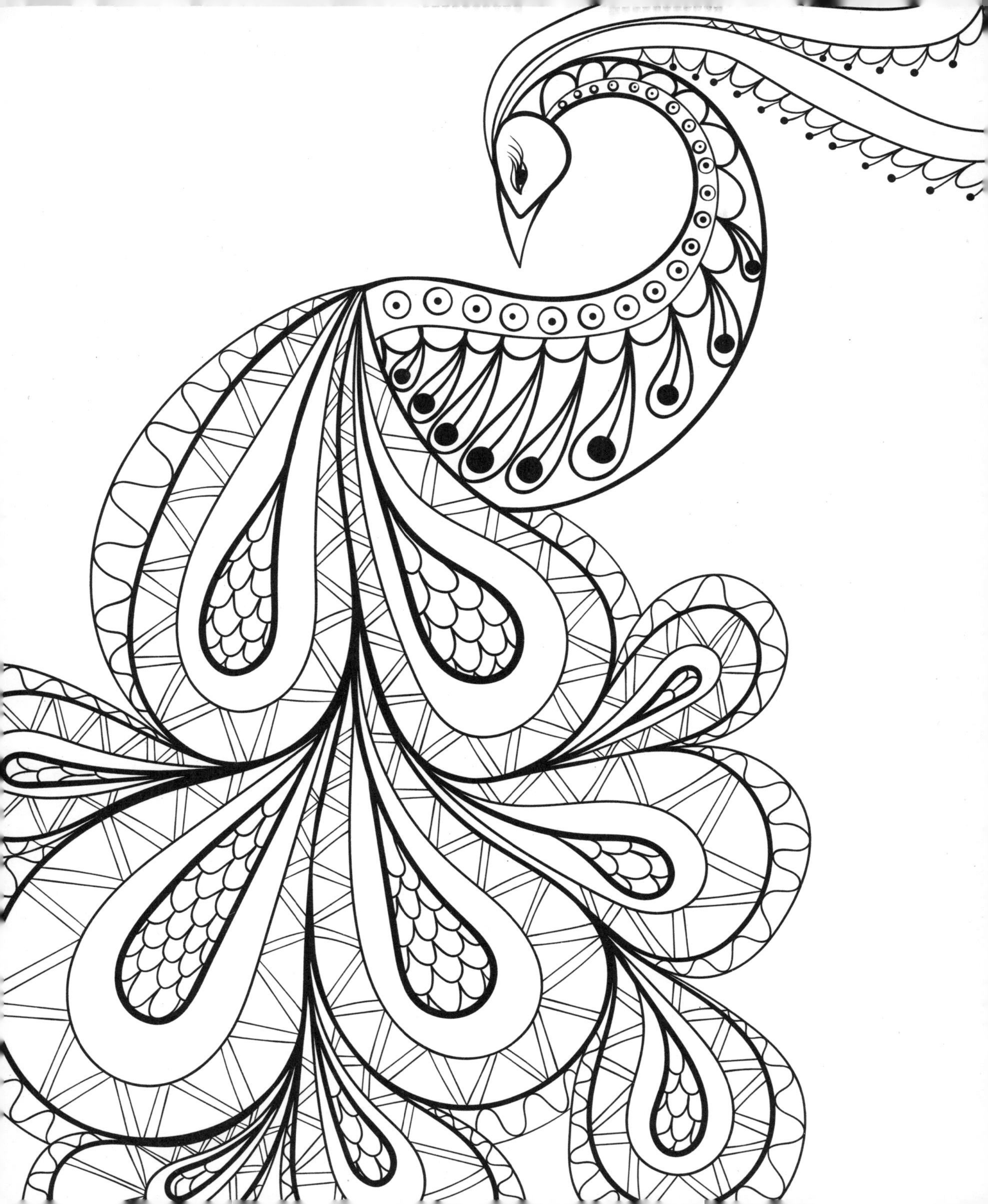

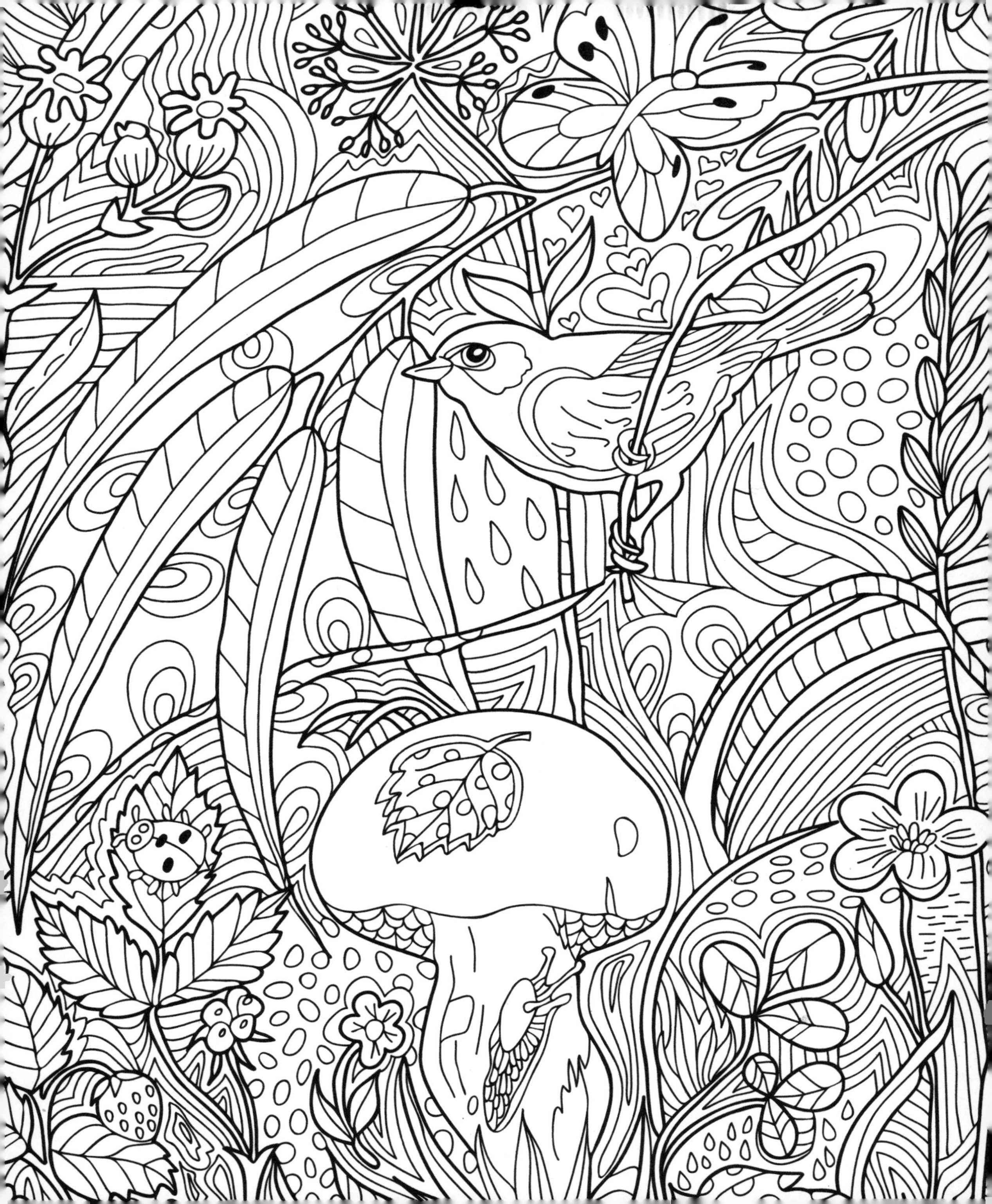

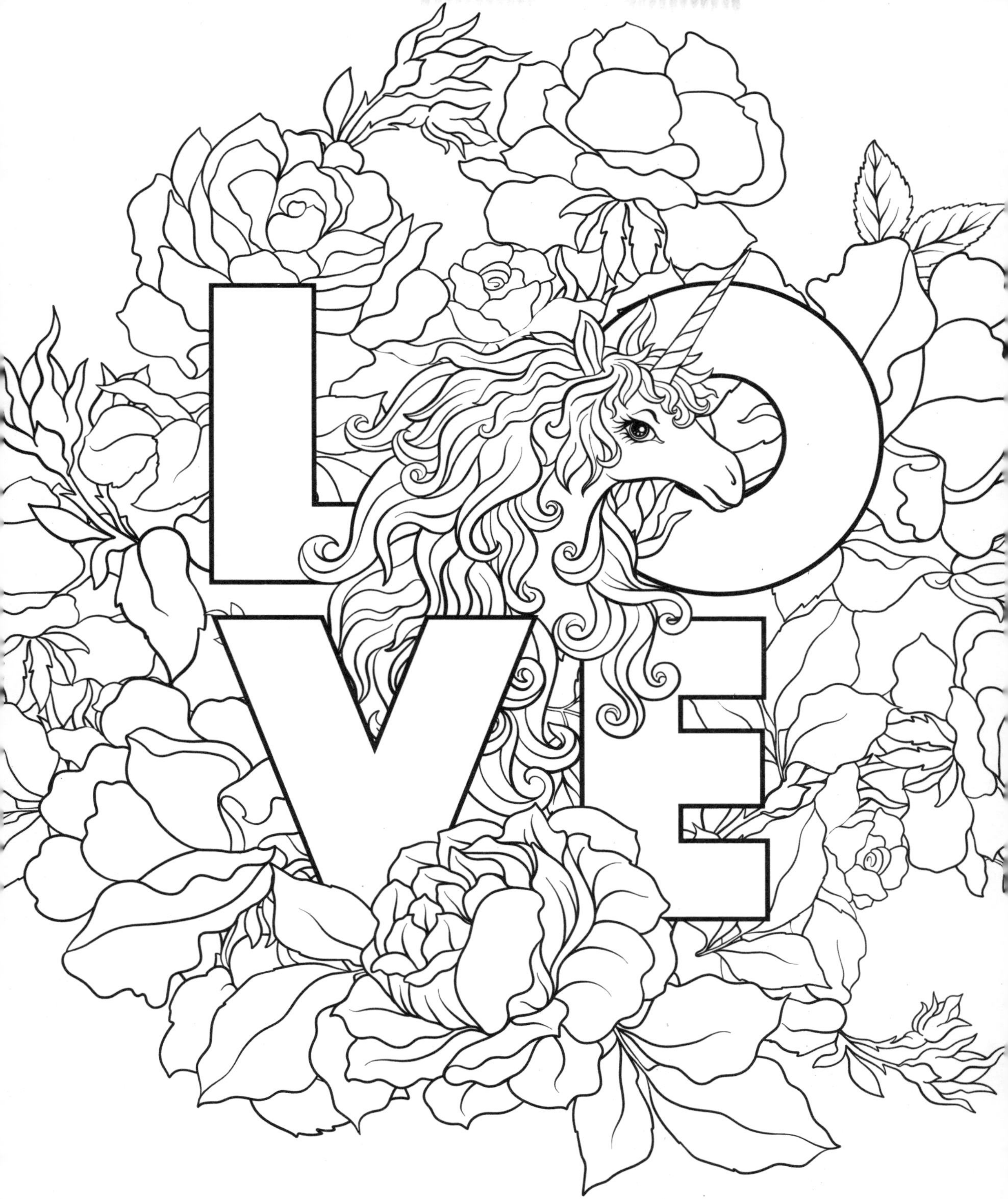
LOVE

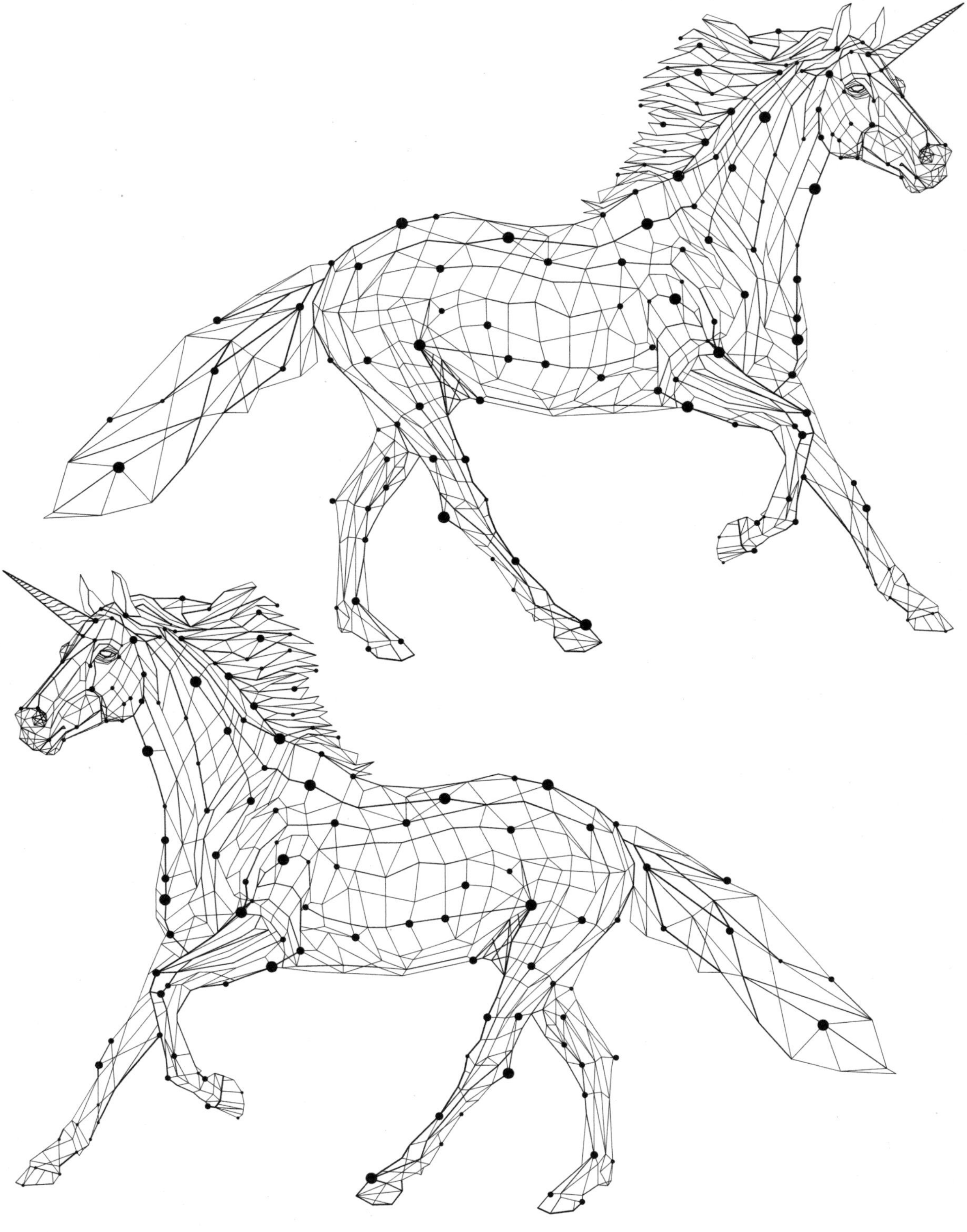

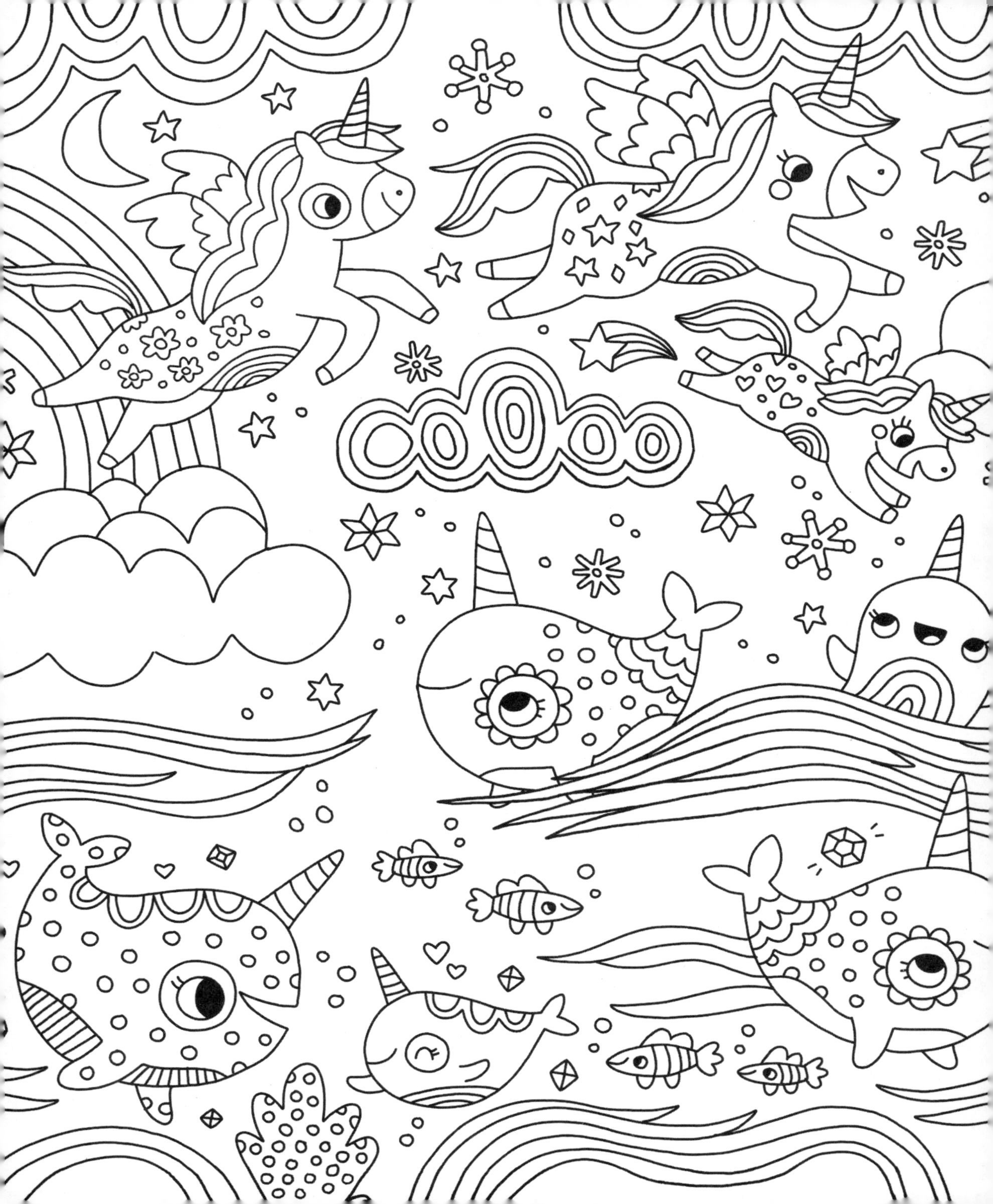

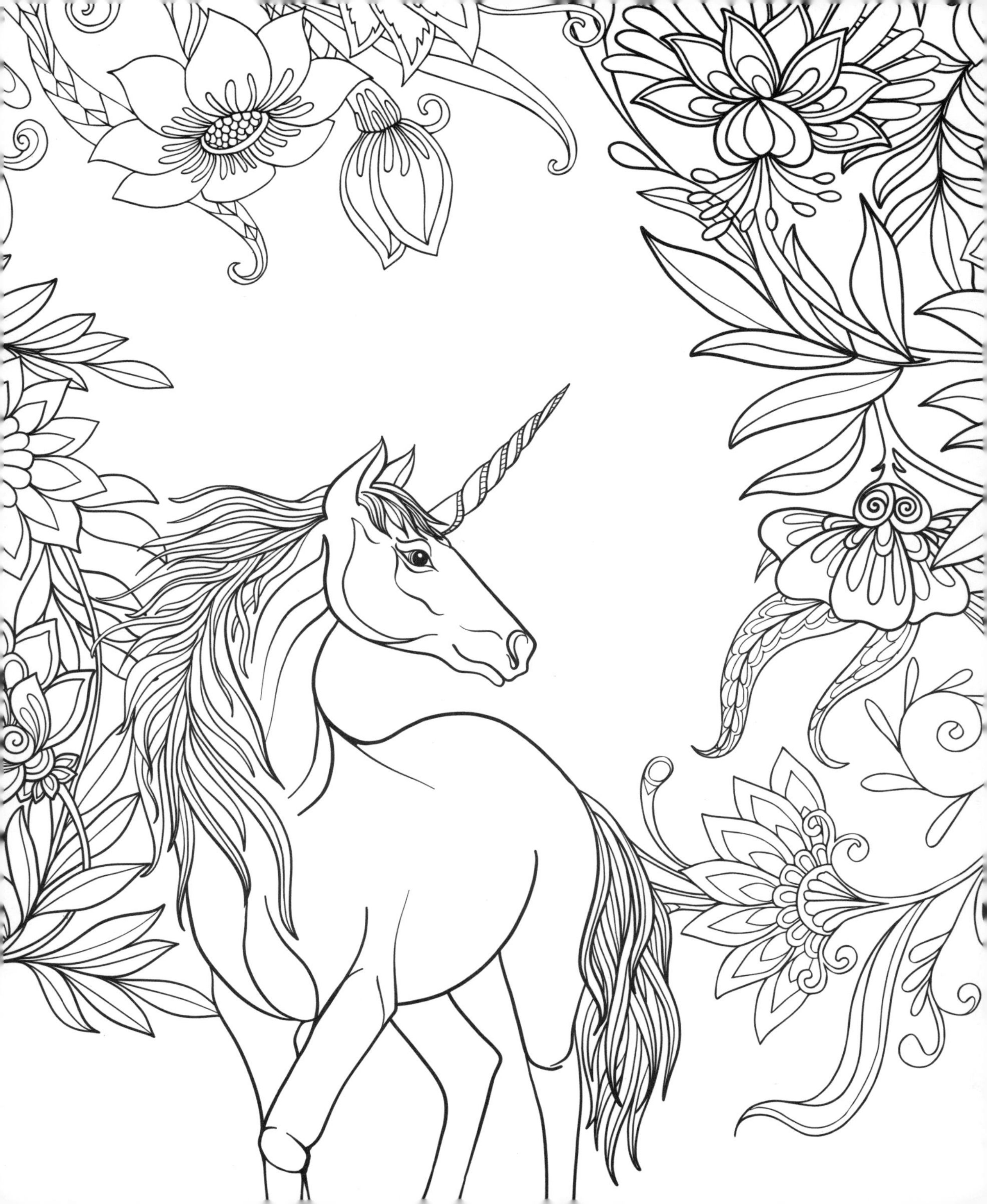

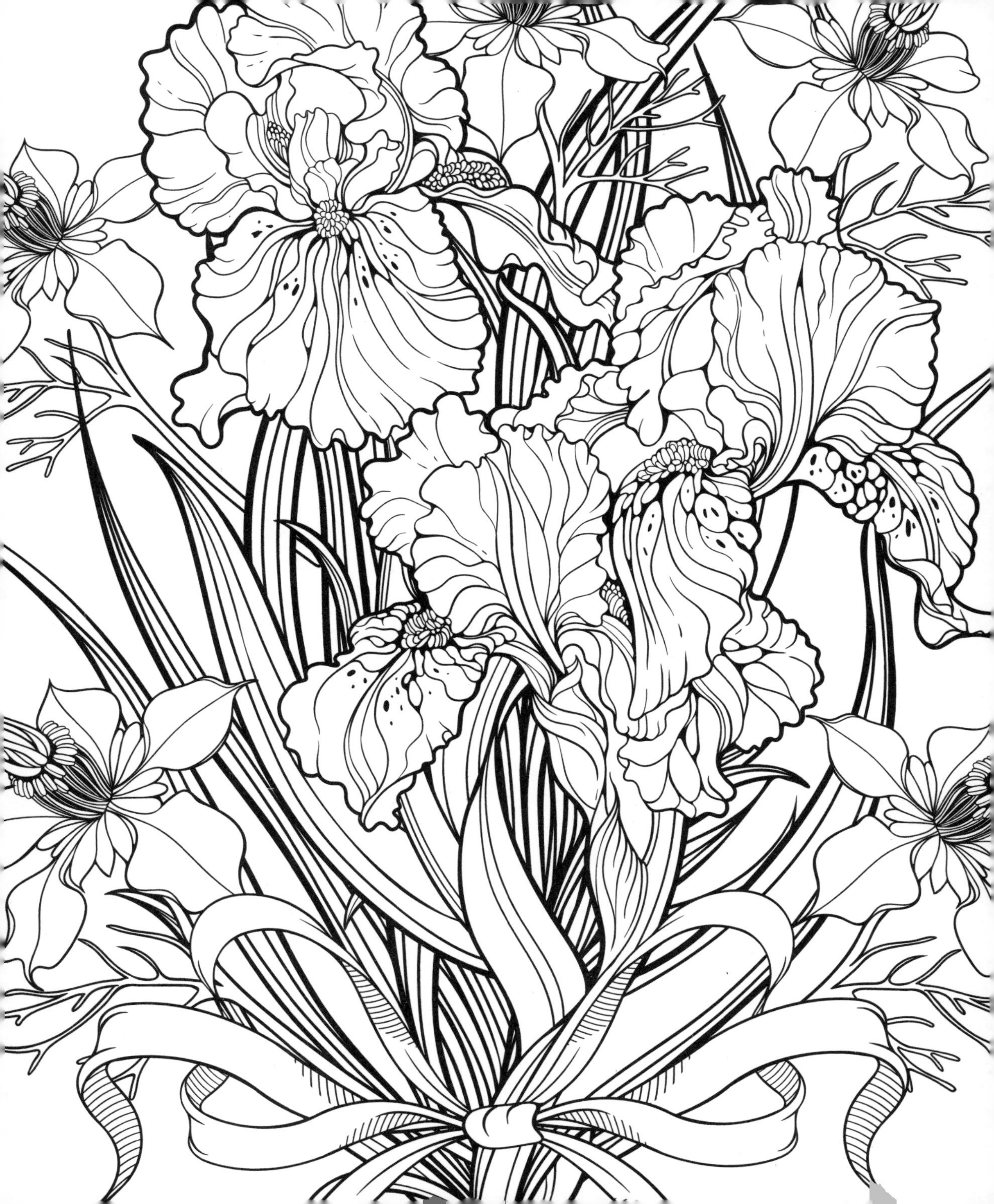

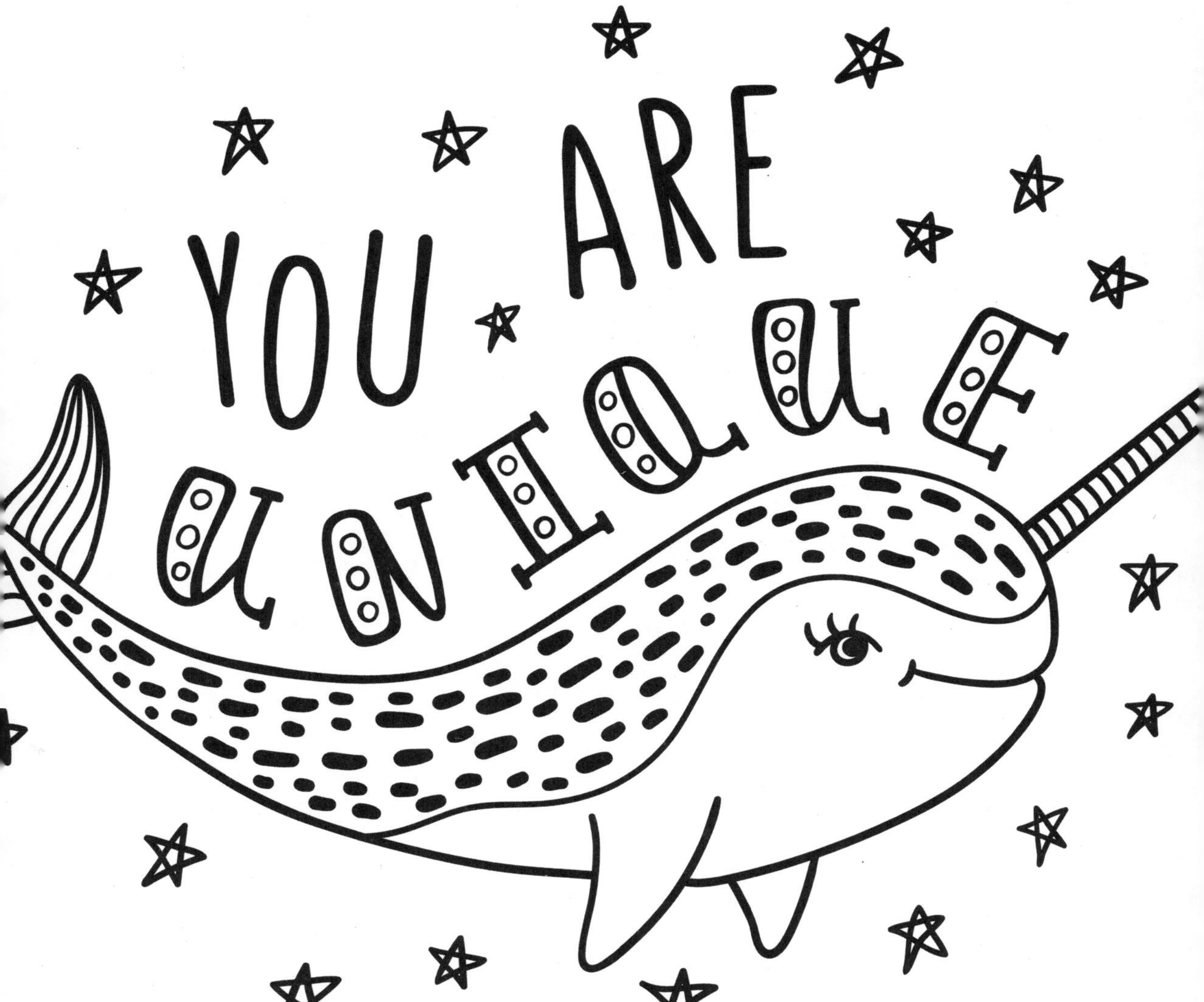
YOU ARE
UNIQUE

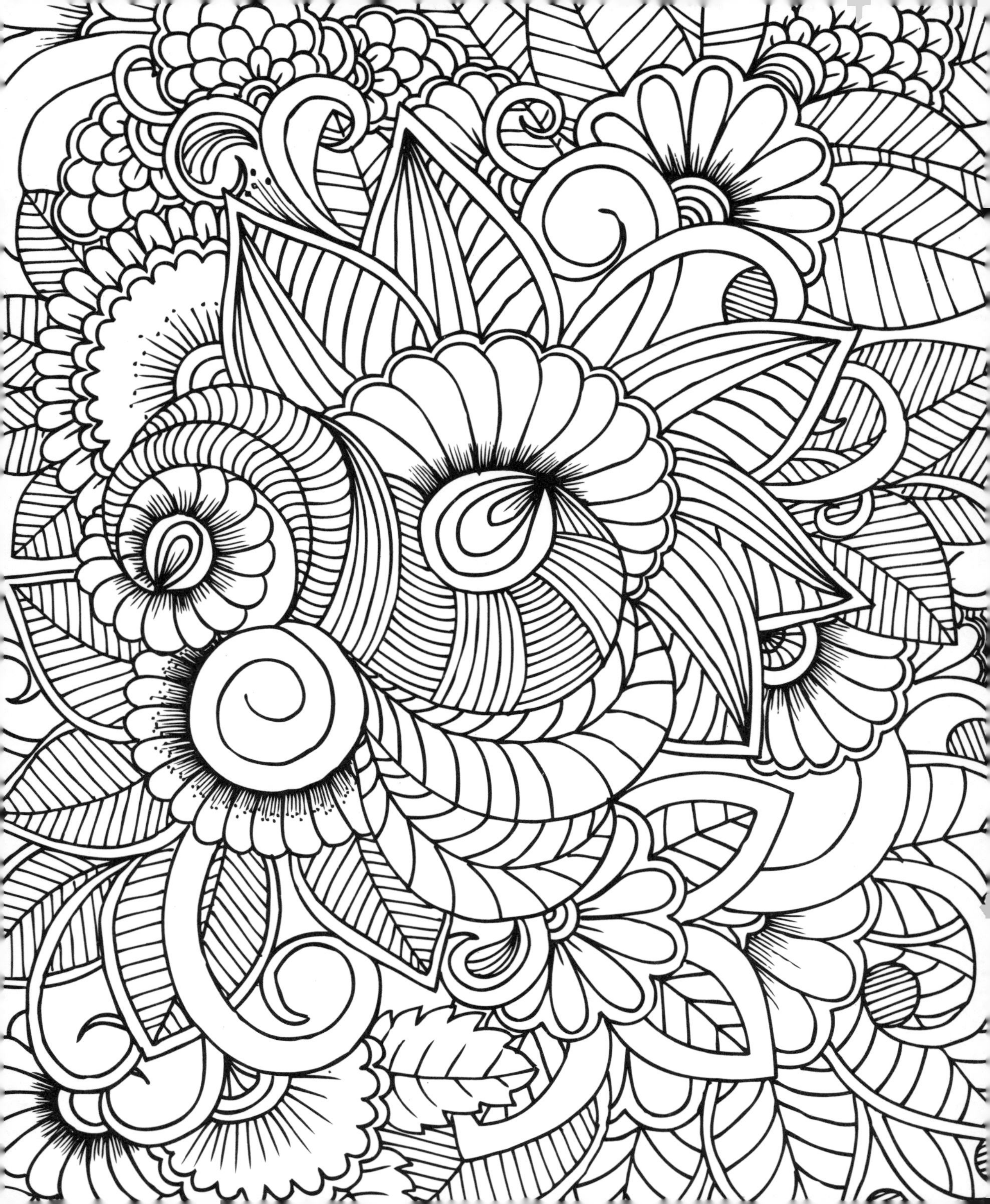

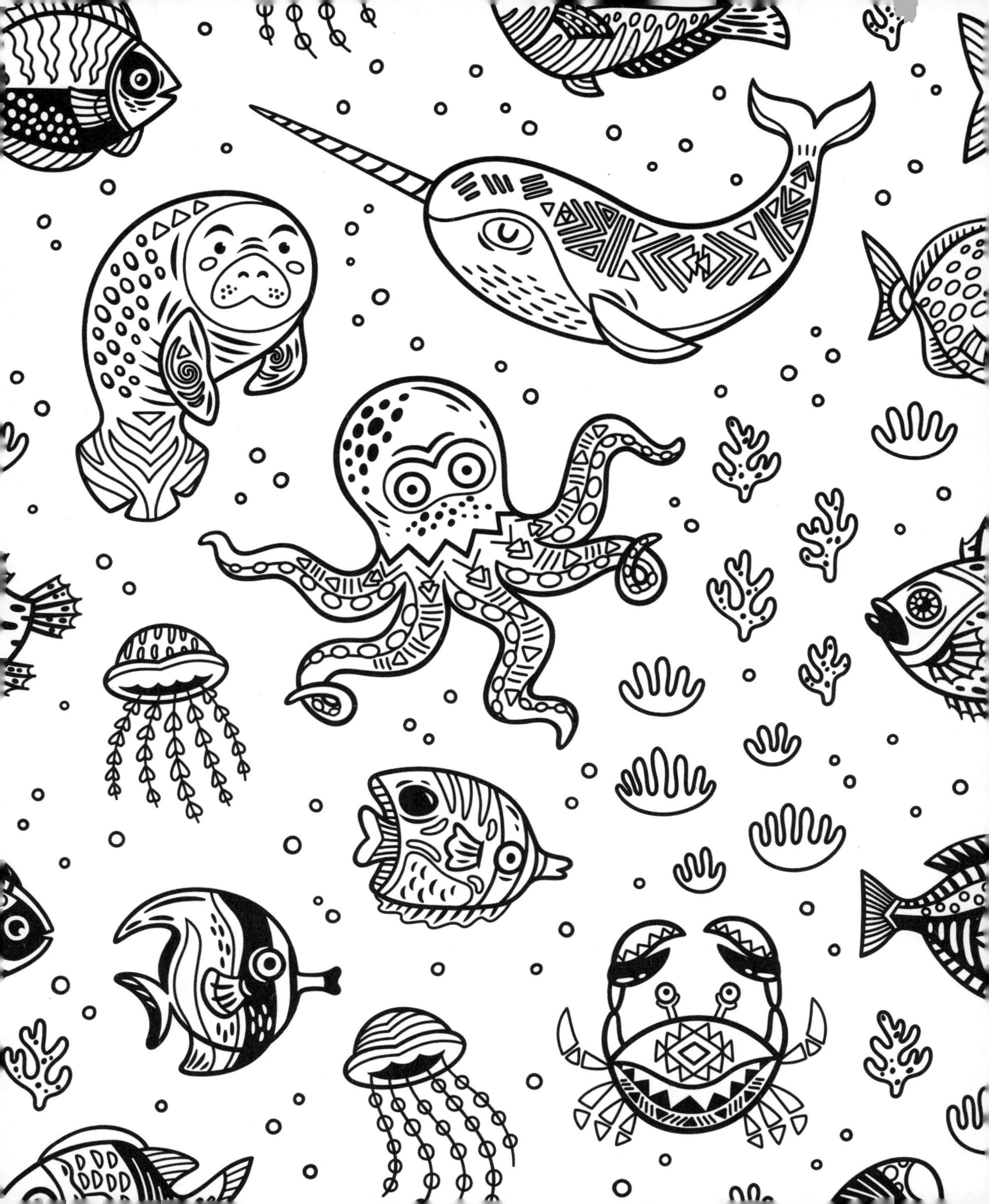

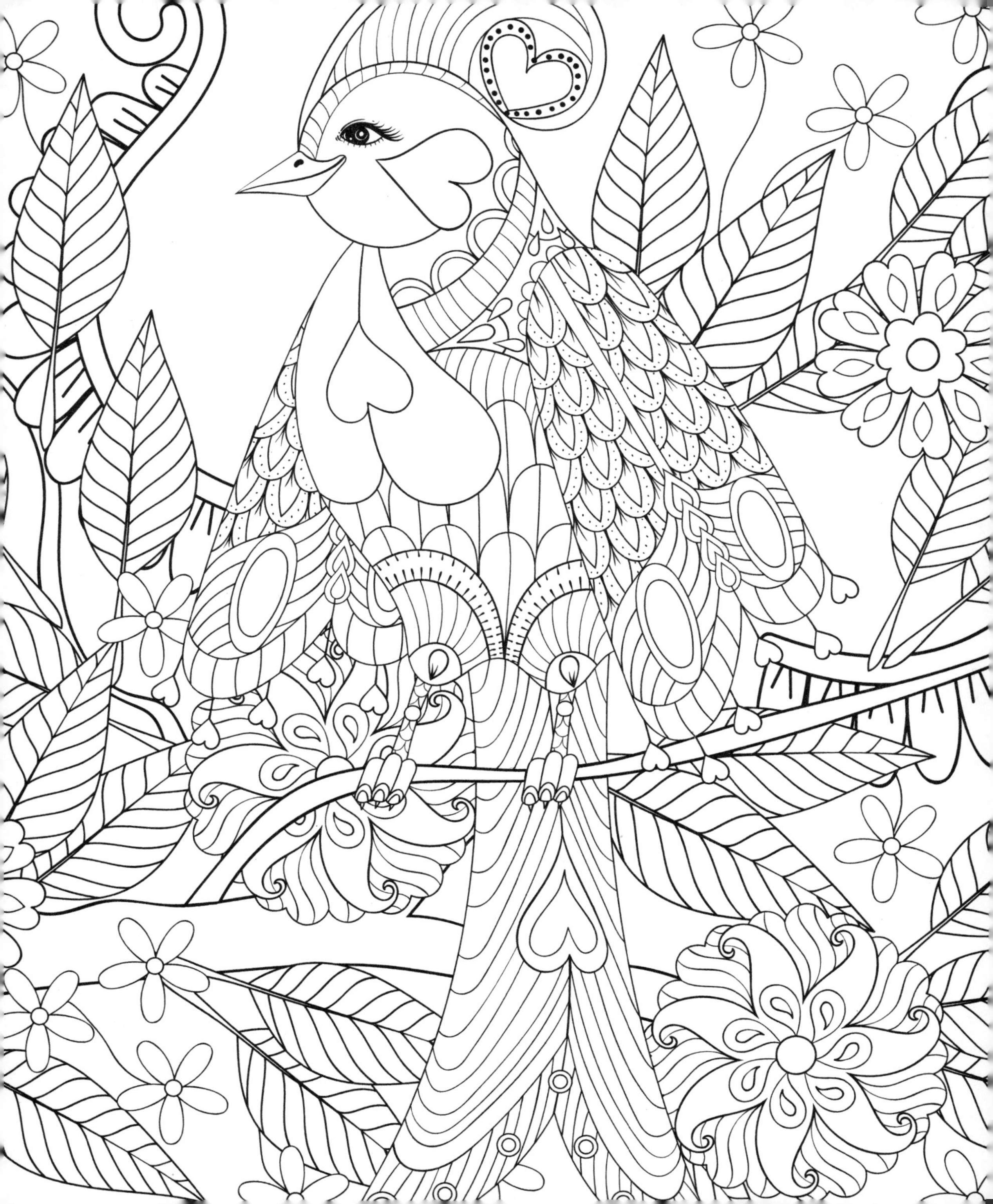

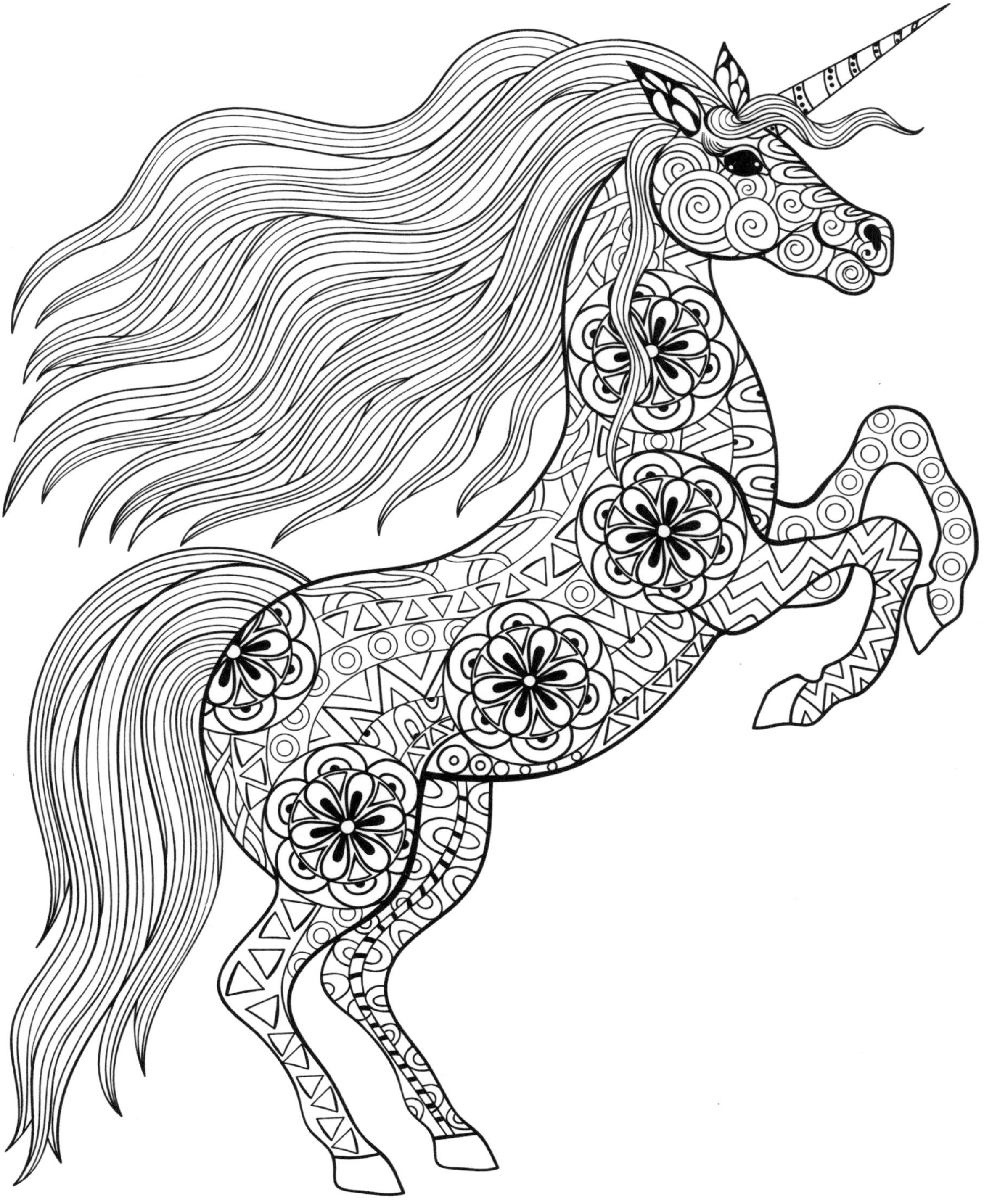

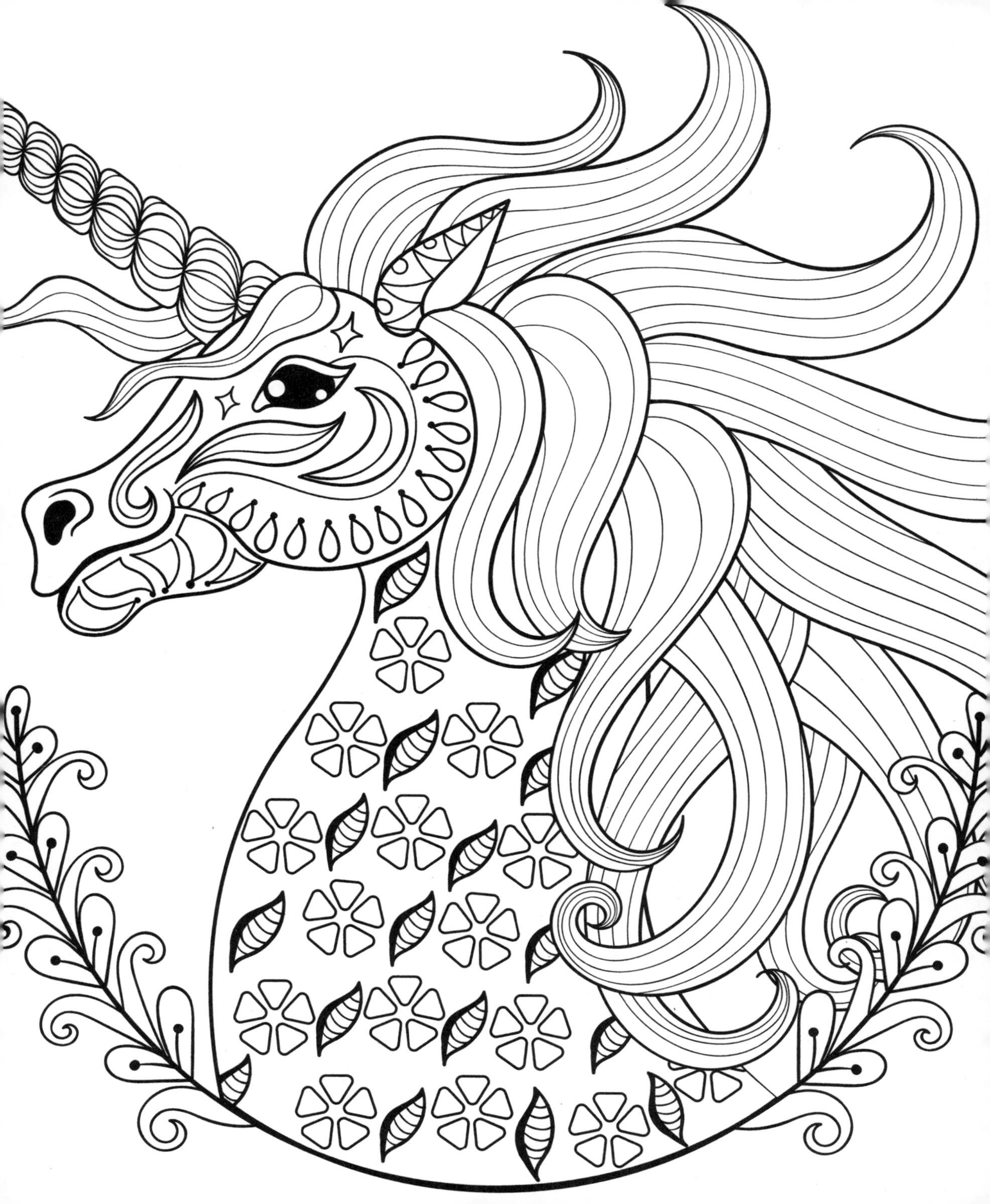

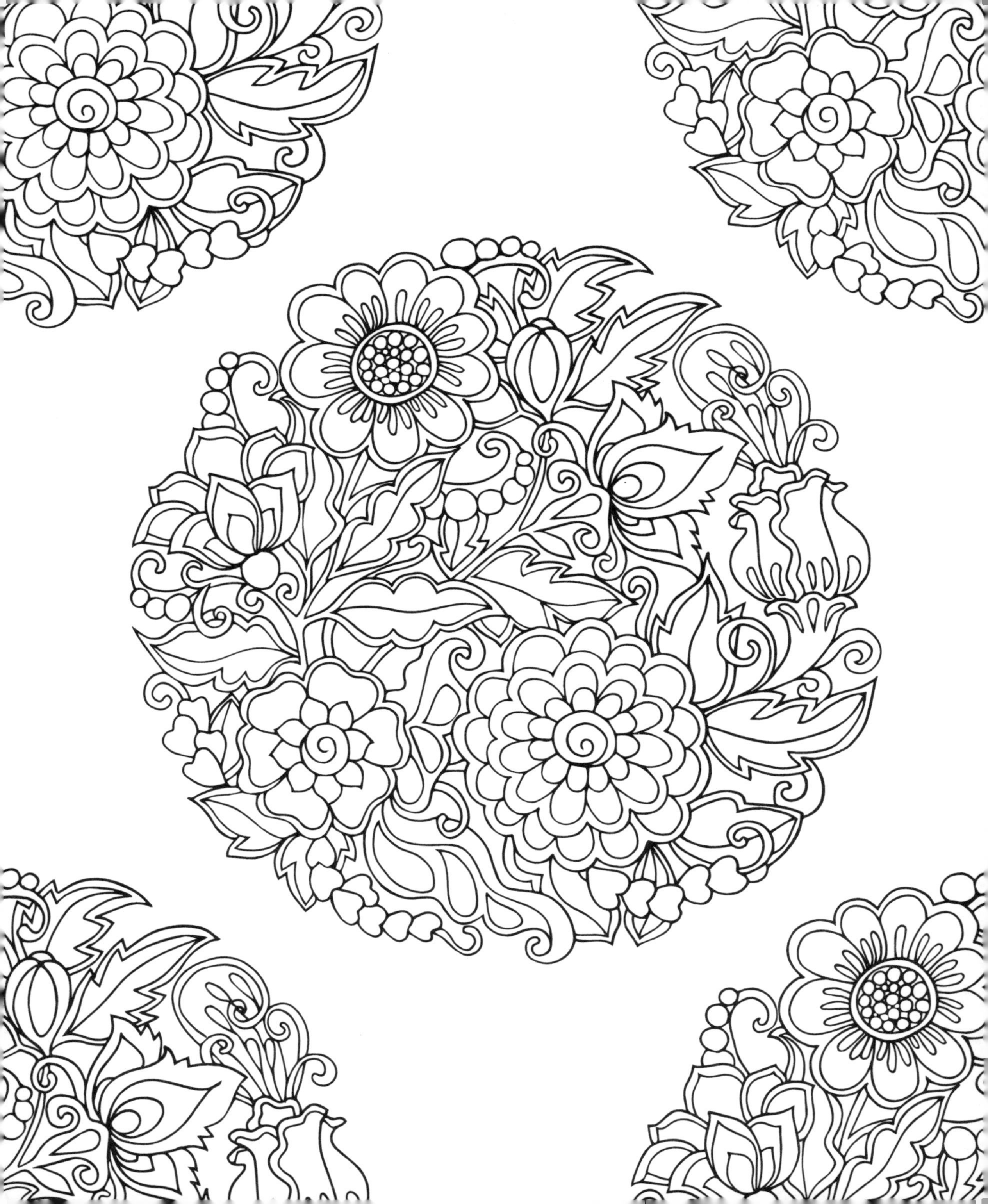

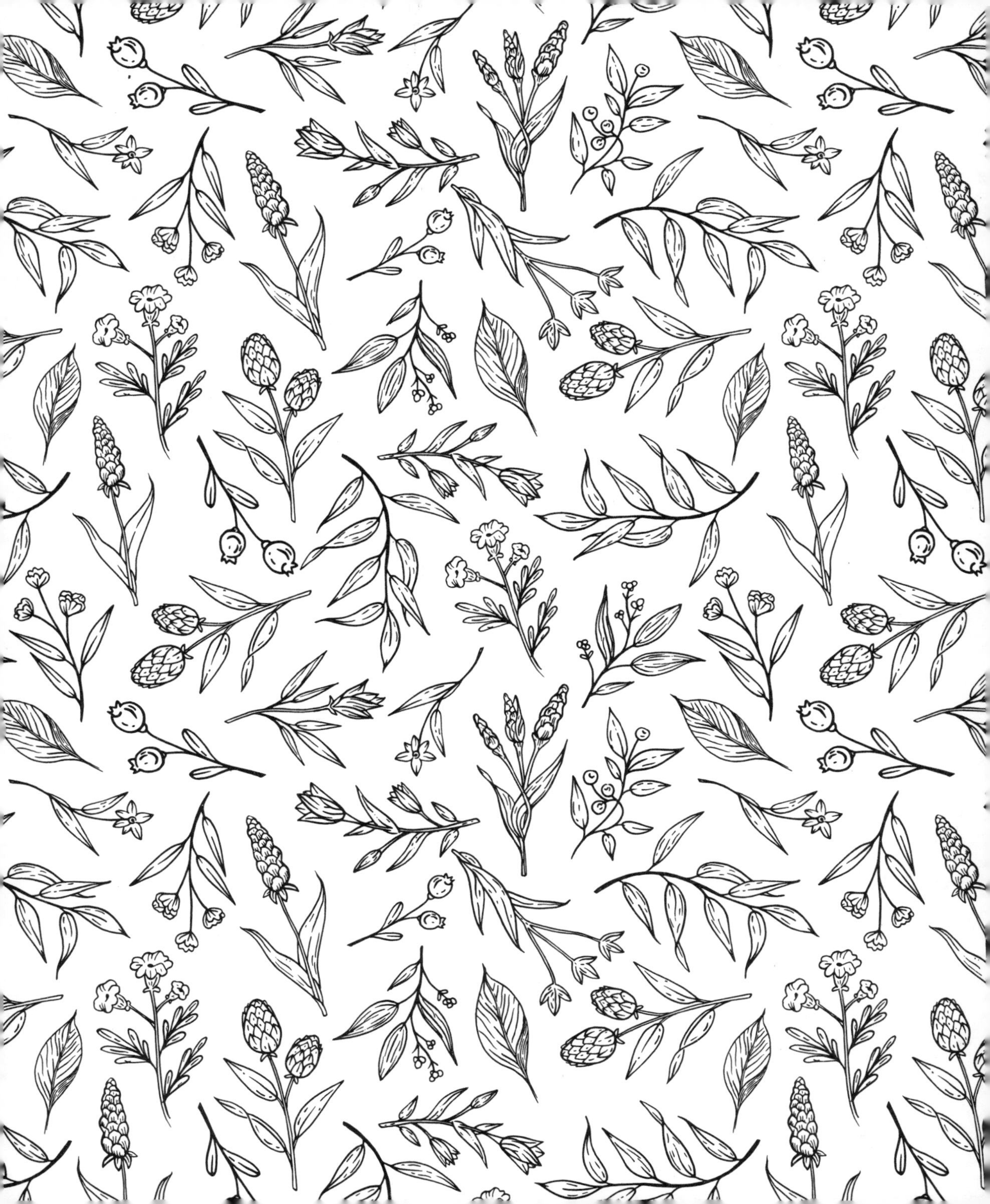

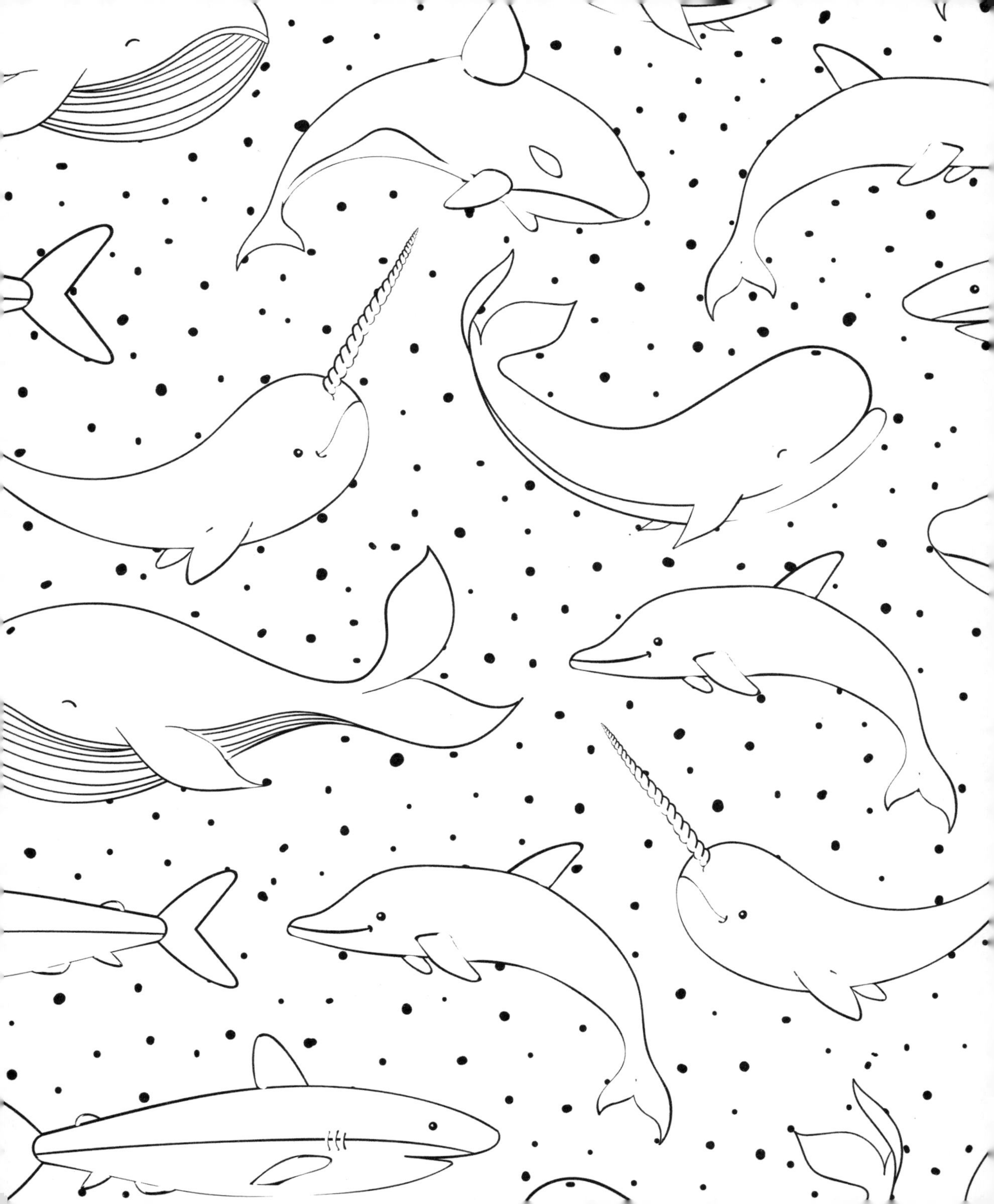

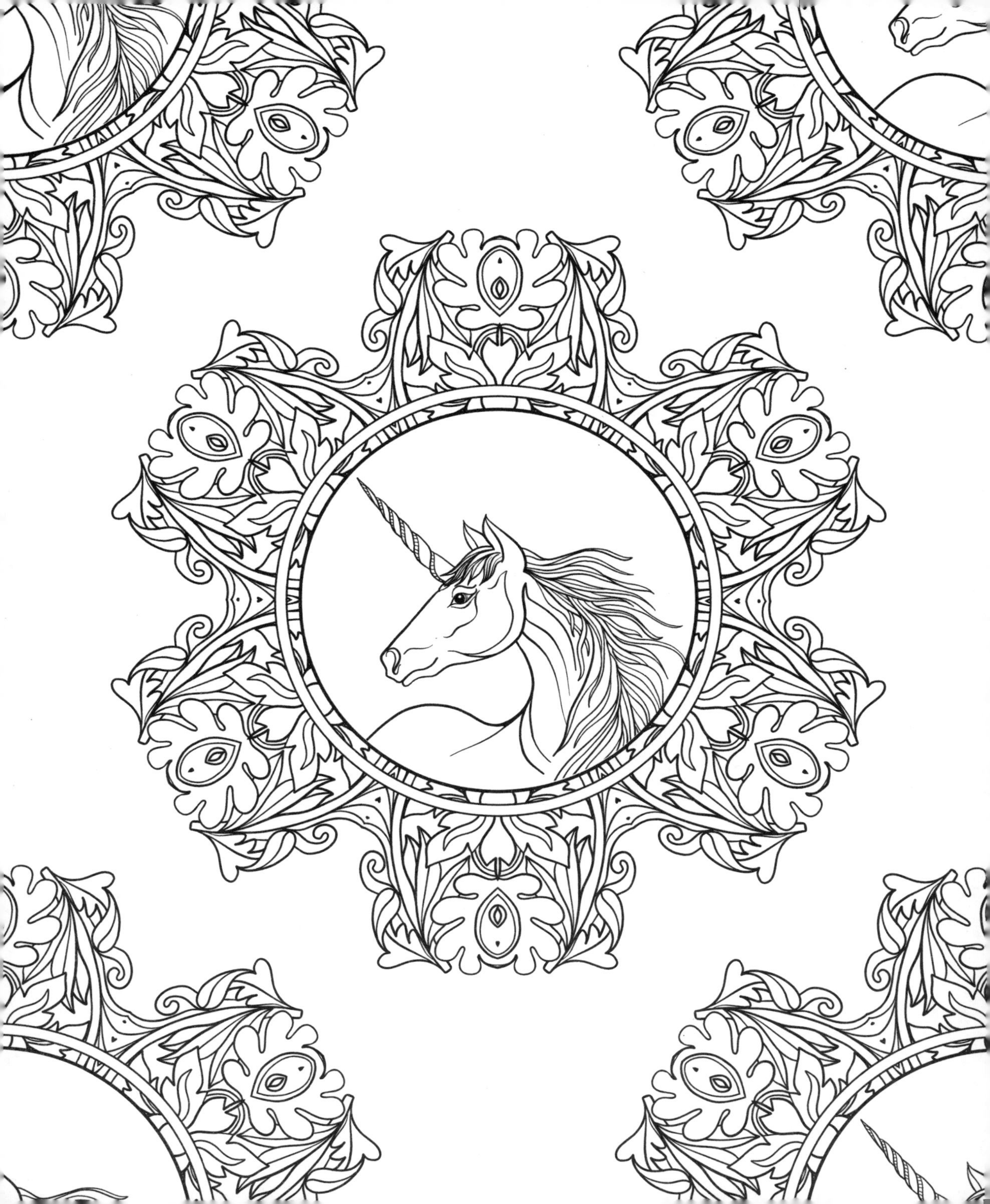

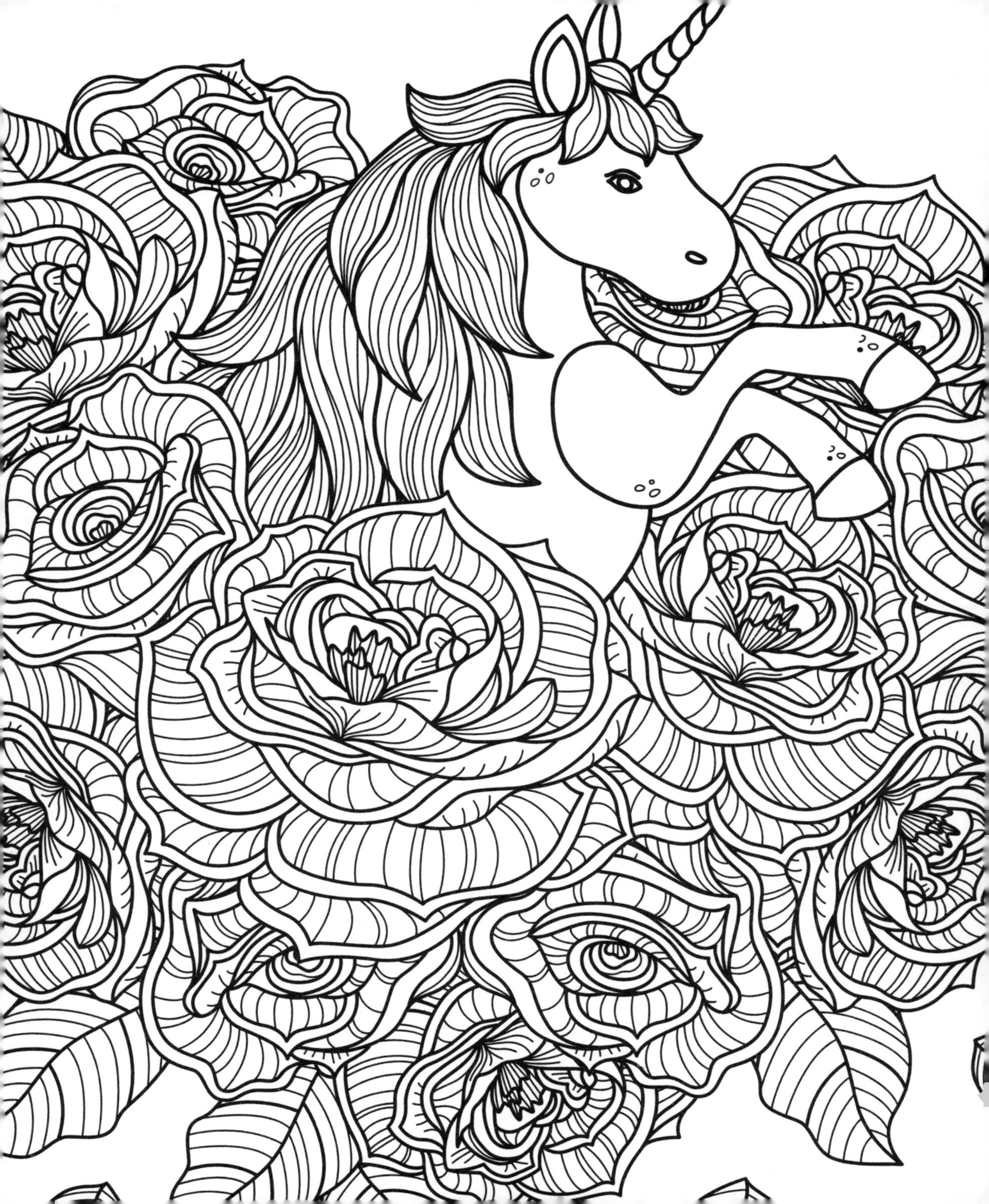

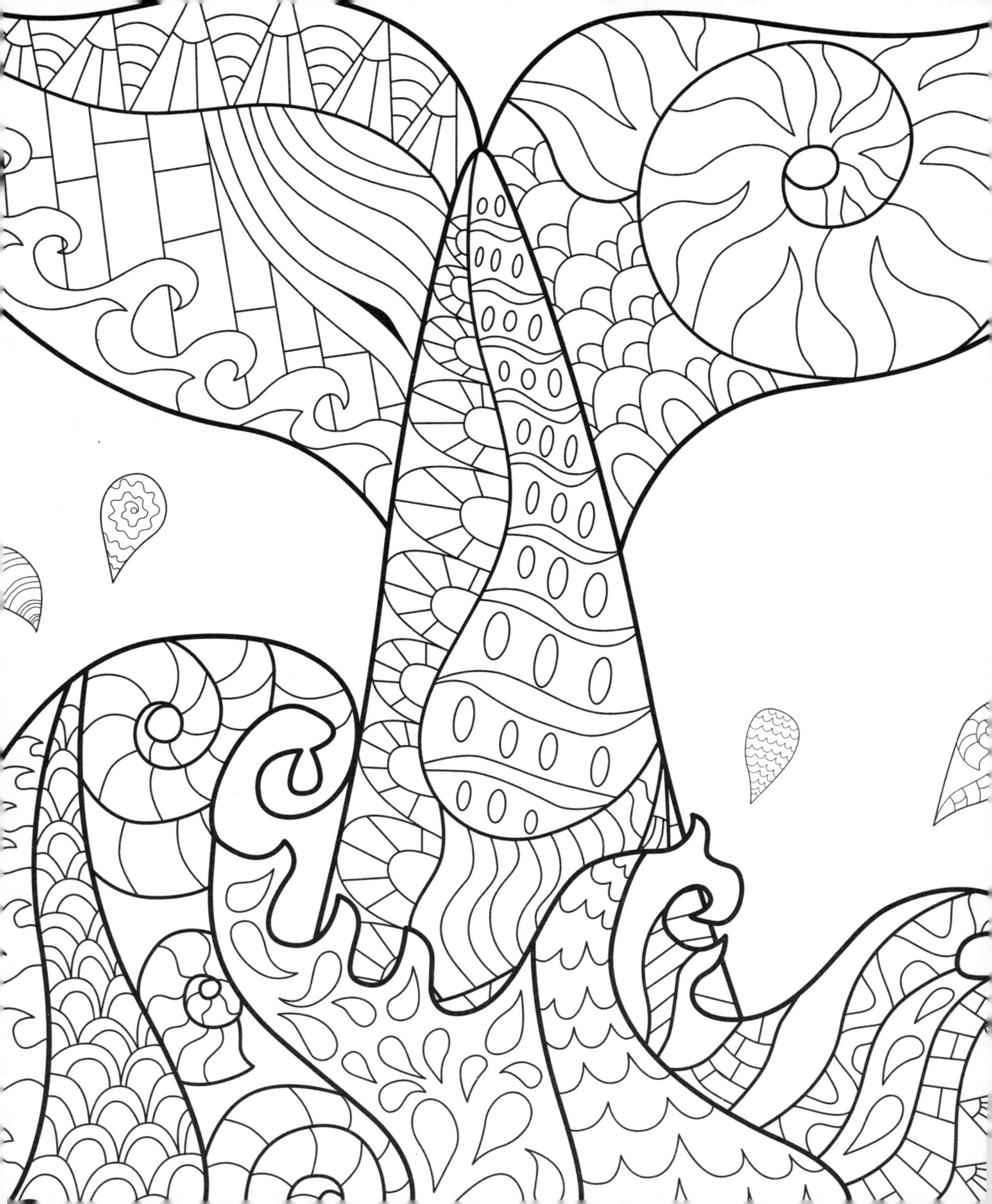

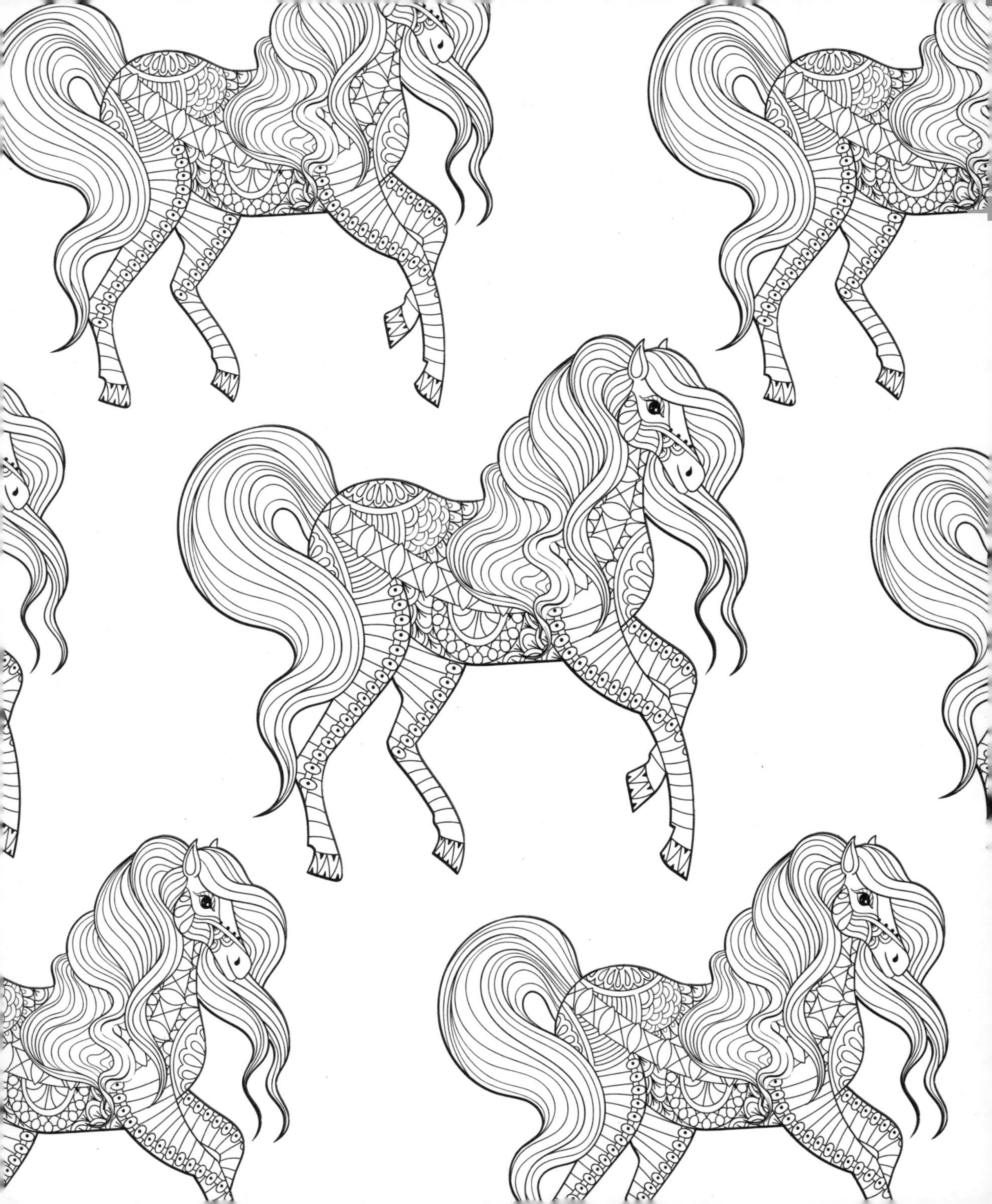

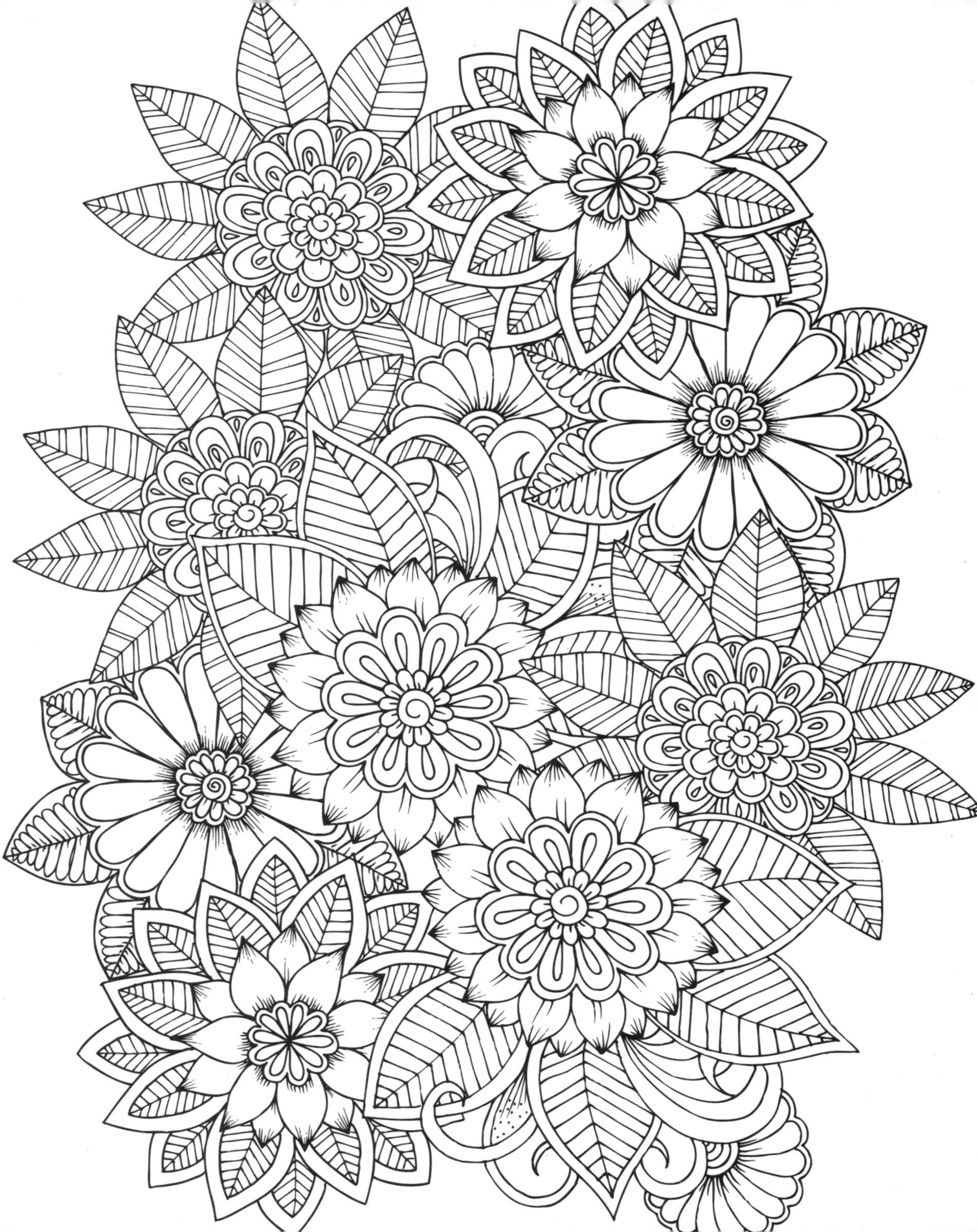

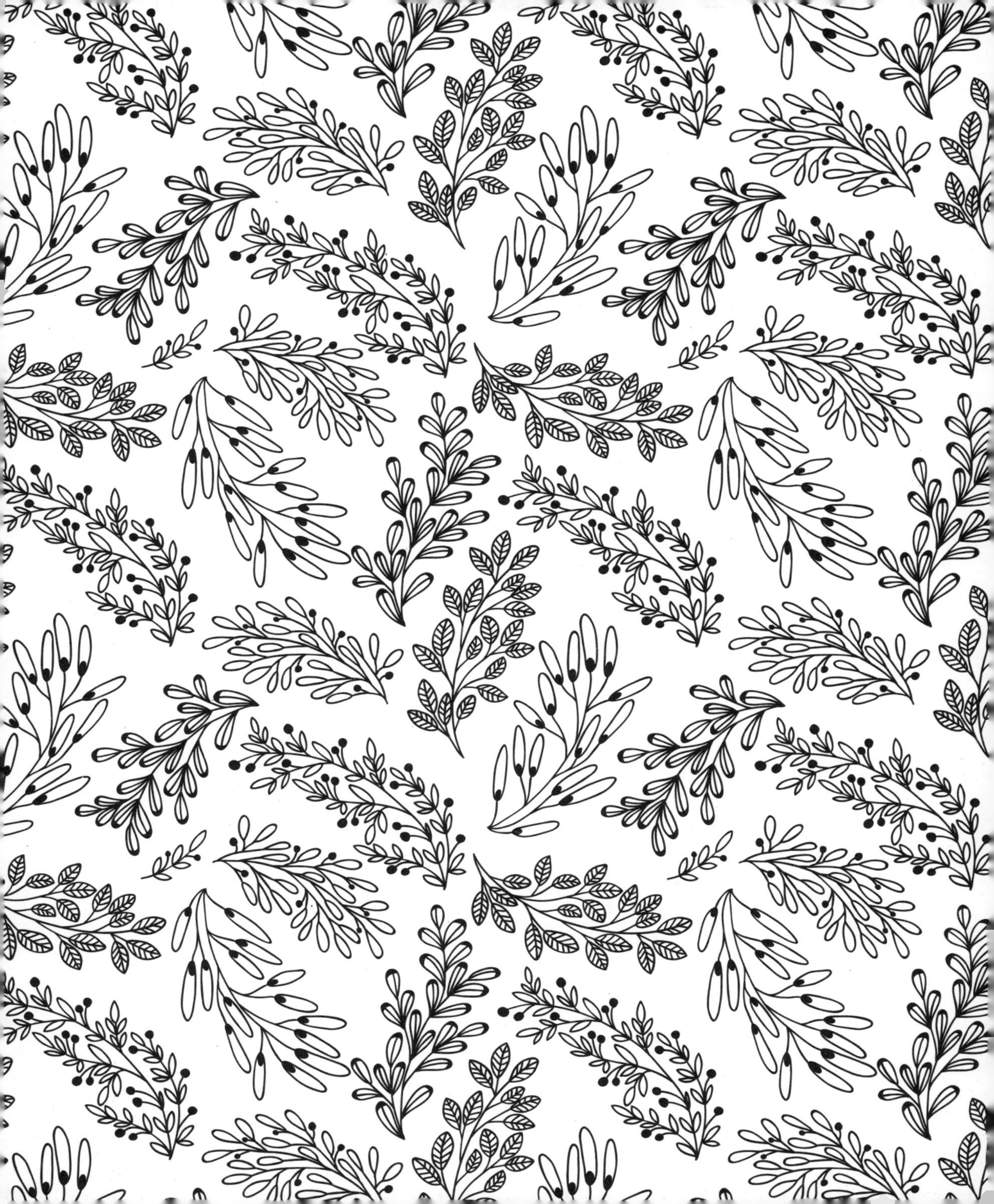

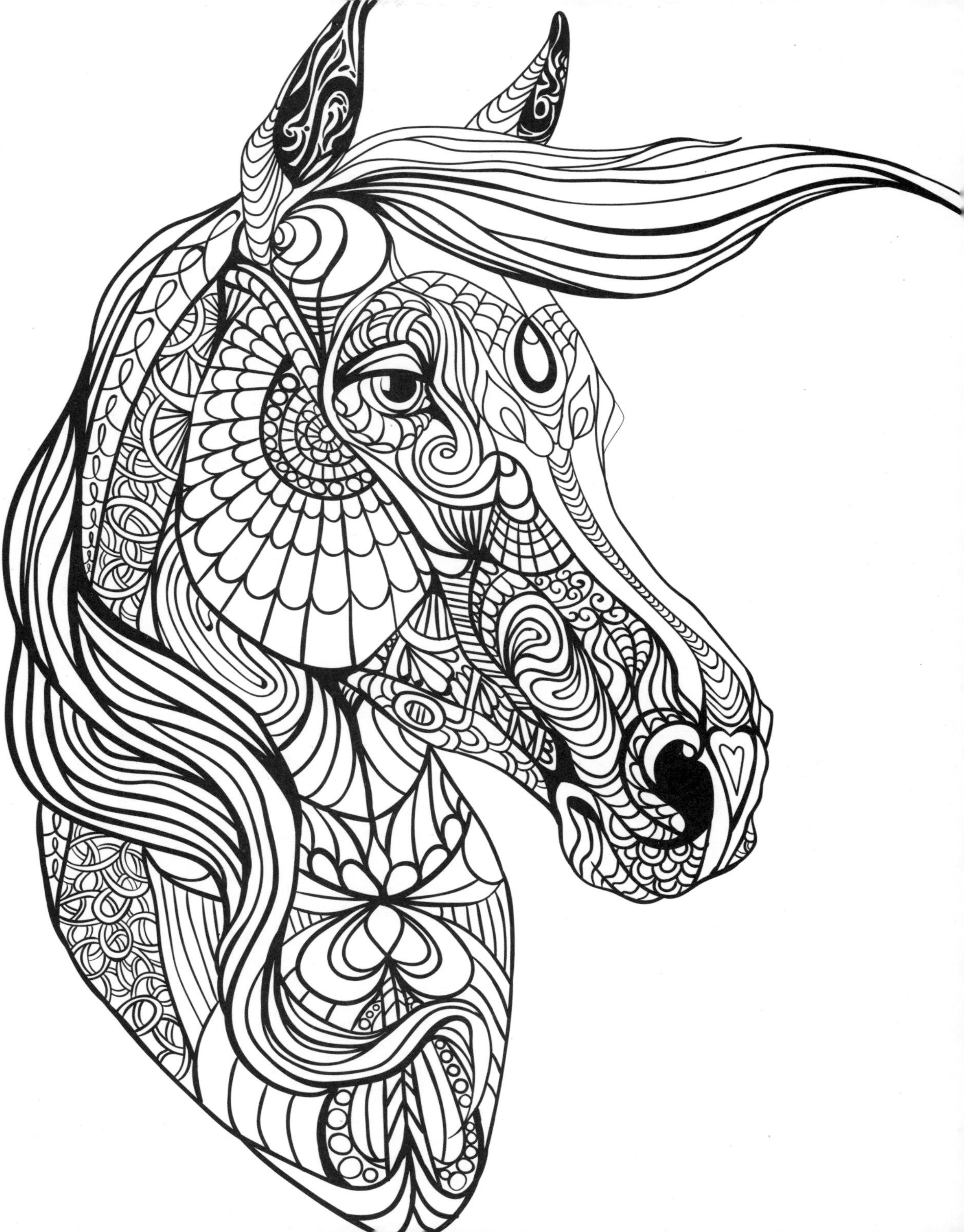

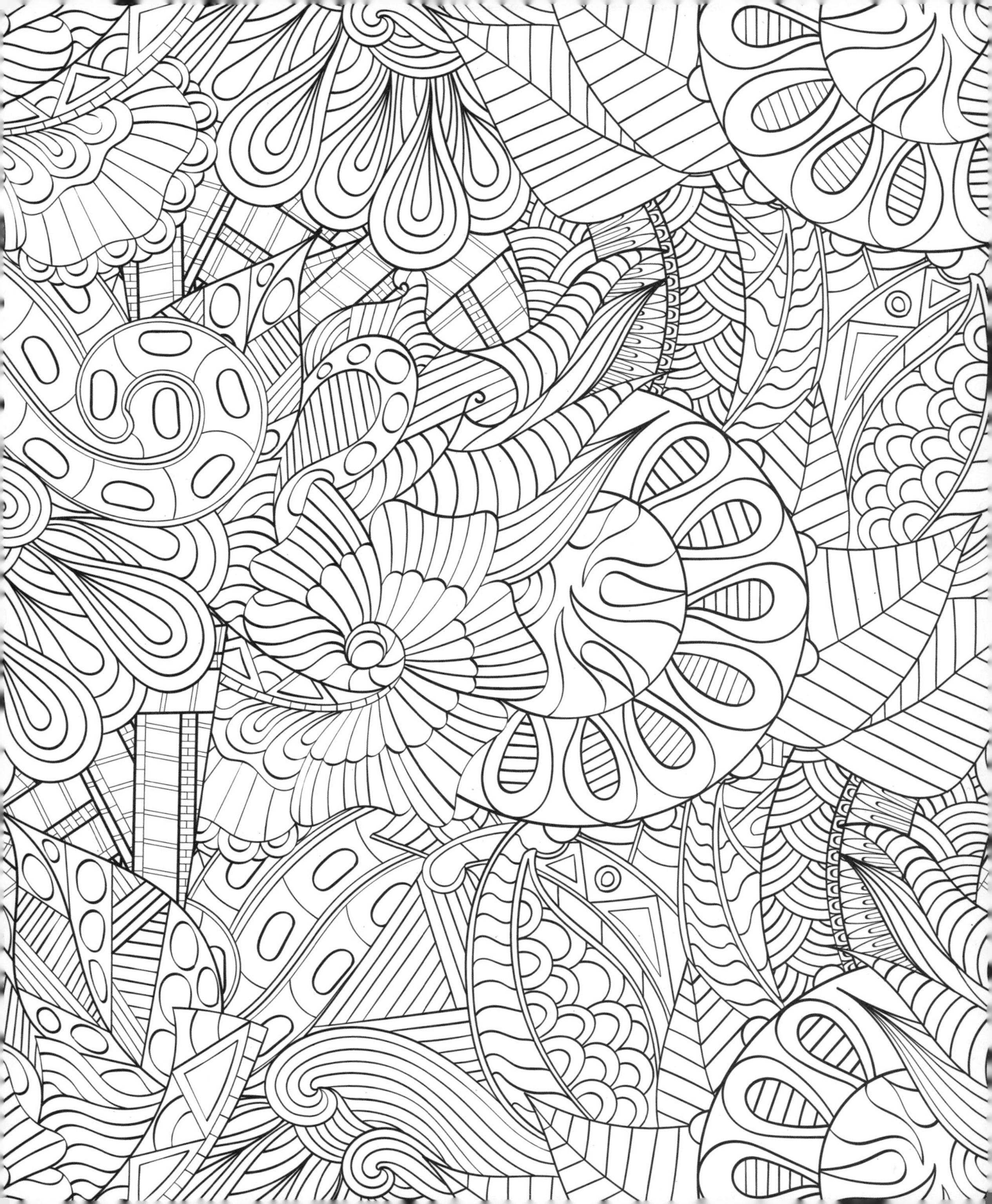

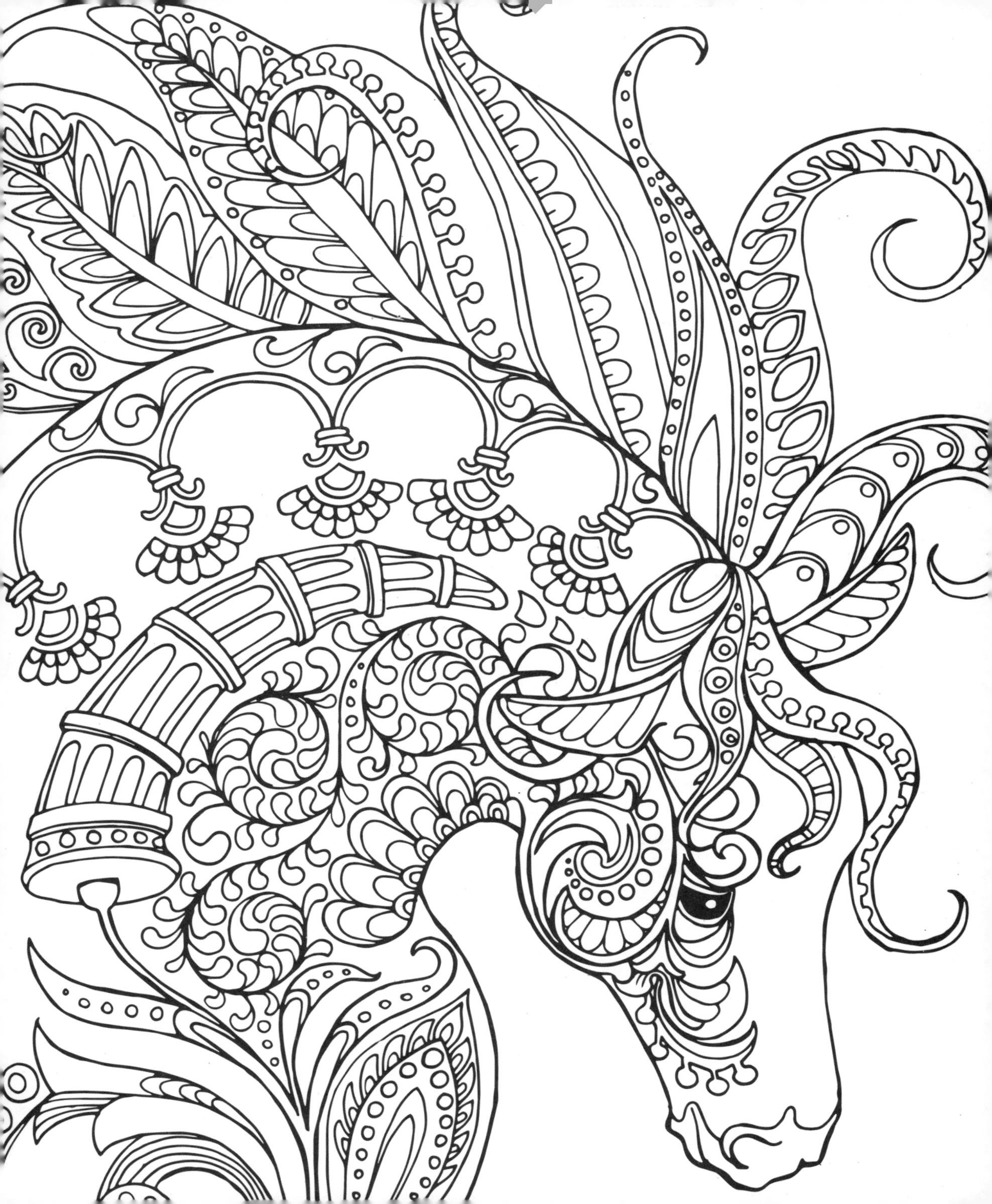

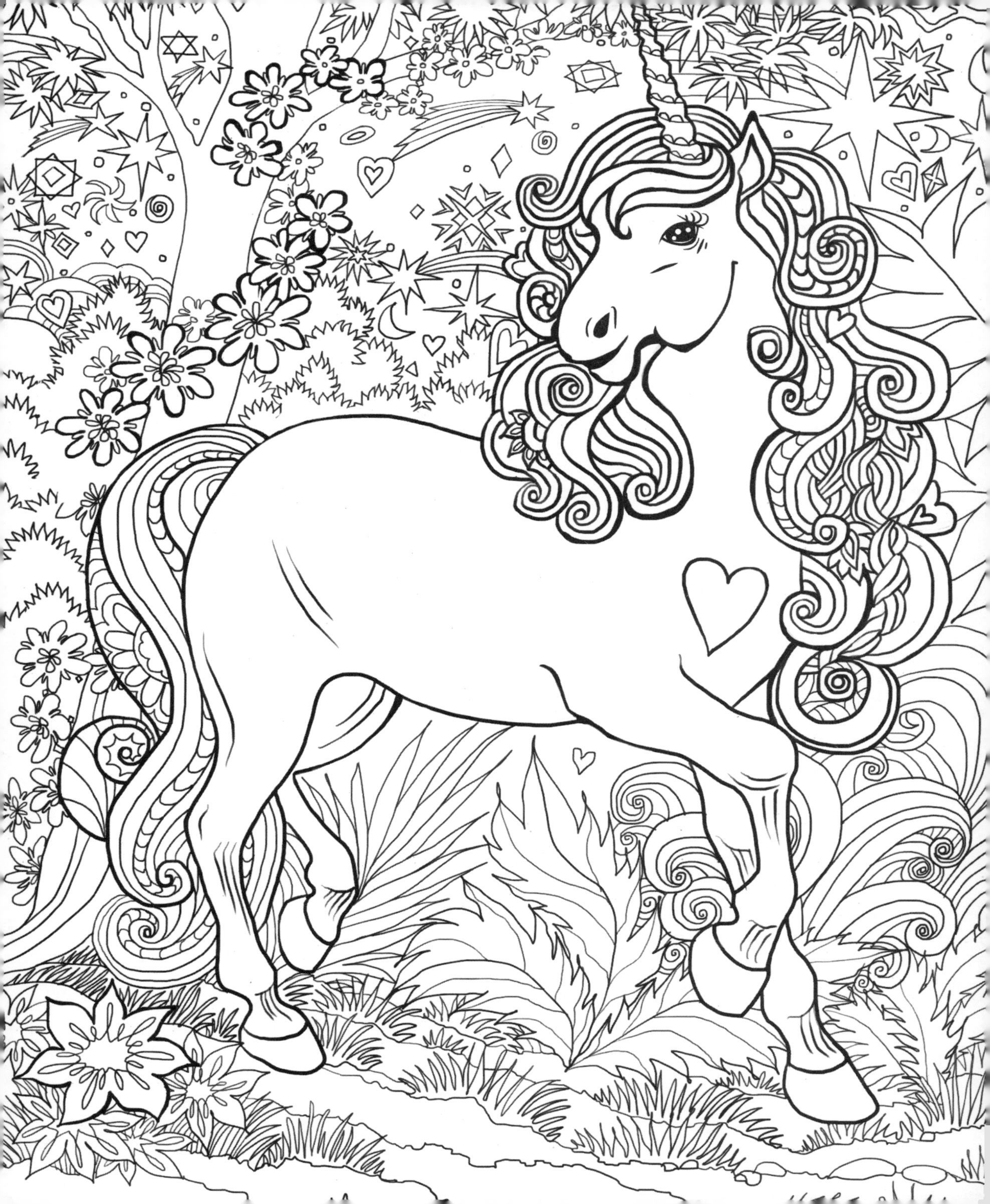

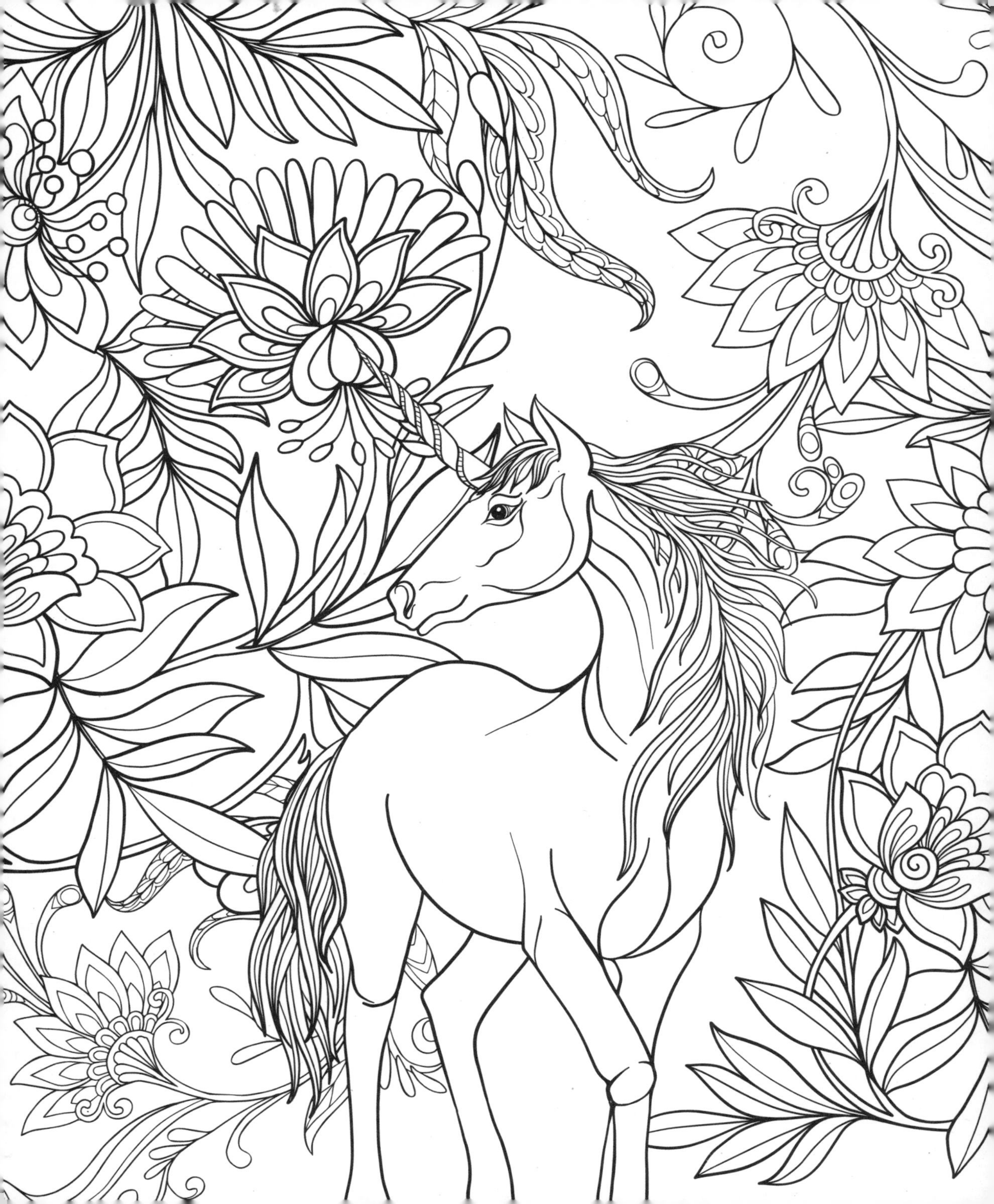